The Genius of a People

The Genius of a People

*What The Scottish Enlightenment
Taught our Founding Fathers*

Robert W. Galvin

To order additional copies of this book, contact:
Xlibris Corporation
1-888-795-4274
www.Xlibris.com
Orders@Xlibris.com

40513

CONTENTS

Why This Book?

In the mid-1990s I discovered a major void in my knowledge of American history. It is revealed on the very first page of the body of this book.

When, by study, I filled the void to my initial satisfaction, it became the central message of five extemporaneous after-dinner speeches requested of me by old friends. The relatively large audiences were the better educated of our citizenry. Each speech was news to all. The attendees were laudatory, grateful to know, much surprised, and often dumbfounded that all of us were never informed.

The way that I found my way to the mid-1990s discovery became, to many, almost as appealing a story as the main focus of this book. Finding my way started with the two hundredth anniversary of the Declaration of Independence which raised the questions, "How does one celebrate? March in a parade? Hold a banquet? Publish ads?" These responses seemed insufficient.

Long before 1976 I was fascinated by the founding process, particularly the founding of our corporation by my father. It dawned on me that a "celebrative" formal study of the founding of our nation would be rewarding for a multiage gathering of our family.

After all, the Declaration of Independence was a literal preamble to the constitutional launching of our country.

These thoughts set me to outlining an agenda for six monthly home dinner meetings. The topics selected were the Declaration itself, the Articles of Confederation, the Constitution, the Federalist Papers, the anti-Federalist Papers, and slavery.

Professors were engaged as proctors. Reading was prepared for each of the sixteen members of the family. Discussants respected the "one voice at a time" format during the four-hour gatherings that yielded in-depth, inspiring inputs and insights by all participants.

Earlier public policy lessons imparted to me were equivalent stimulators. These focused on the Constitution and the Federalist Papers and the scholarship of Dr. Robert Goldwin, then a member of the faculty of the University of Chicago, and Dr. Martin Diamond (deceased), then of the Claremont College group, who was preeminently knowledgeable about the Federalist Papers.

Bob Goldwin, a friend over the years and a recent resident scholar of the American Enterprise Institute, Washington, D.C., shared with me inspiring conversations in the 1960s, as well as his many texts over later years, detailing the thinking and the interplay of our extraordinary constitutional authors. About the same era, Martin Diamond was guest of honor at adult dinner parties in our home where we encouraged evening-long lively debates of self-appointed Federalists and anti-Federalists.

Much of those scholars' influence is reflected in paragraphs on pages 89-93 in this book. With the passing of decades, I cannot separate what expressions in those paragraphs may have been fashioned at my rhetorical initiation versus others that should be expressly attributable to Robert Goldwin and/or Martin Diamond. If, as is likely, I have retained and expressed here any of their thoughtful phrasing of the content that they taught me, it is simply subliminal manifestation of my appreciation for and acknowledgment of their lasting influence.

Ironically, none of these personal teachers or tutors ever mentioned the Scottish Enlightenment. My "antenna" was always tuned for the new. Luckily, I simply stumbled over the idiom and a hint that Americans benefited.

The administration and librarians at the Newberry Library in Chicago were invaluable by opening their stacks and my eyes to this big story. Friends sought me out with rare sources.

Many credentialed scholars portray and examine the Scottish movement and its individuals. I have read them admiringly. However, very few of them bring out the link in the thinking between the two countries. A finite few slip in a sentence, maybe two. A reader has to be keenly alert to catch the connection.

To satisfy friends who insisted on a copy of my (unwritten) speeches, I finally penned an essay, then a supporting essay. But the subject—the consequences of the linkage—deserved more. Hence, this book.

As an active citizen, I hope to share with other citizens what I assert are the equal of any of the other paramount lessons our history can teach. The importance is not simply in the knowing. Extractable principles and guidelines can play an essential and stimulating role in nation building for one or more of today's lesser-developed societies.

The Scottish did it.
Our ancestors did it.
Can others?
With our guidance?

We'll touch on that at the end.

Introduction to the Scottish Enlightenment

This is the story of the genius of a people. In fact, it is the story of the genius of two peoples—the Scottish and the Americans. They meet about AD 1750, after an epic two hundred and fifty years (circa 1500-1750) of unparalleled self-development by the citizens and country of Scotland, resulting in the assembly of the incomparable men of wisdom of the Scottish Enlightenment; and, on the eve of the hastening gatherings of the prospective founders of the United States of America. For the next two hundred and fifty years, *our* country bloomed and eventually flourished in critical part from the practical application of that exceptional shared wisdom.

Did you know there was a Scottish Enlightenment? I didn't. As this book goes to press, most people do not. We are going to correct that oversight right up front.

The Scottish Enlightenment was

- The grandest aggregation for any given time in history of the leading scholars from virtually *all* then existing fields of knowledge
- Thinking together in one locale
- During a single compressed era of time—a decade or two before and after 1750

They and their then all-encompassing intelligence are the centerpiece of this book. You will meet these scholars and their thinking in the middle pages. For now, let your interest be satisfied to learn just one prime influence. By the time Madison, Monroe, and Jefferson were sixteen years of age, they and others were being instructed and inspired by a product of the Enlightenment—the many Scottish clerics who were arriving in the colonies to evangelize, often needing to earn their keep by tutoring. Tutoring what? The Enlightenment's useful thinking and textural sources.

The Naming of America

As the curtain rose for the second half of the millennium, AD 1500, a myriad of transcending advances and challenges were emerging throughout earth's developing societies. This book—the *untold* story of the founding of the United States centuries later—pivots off three of those then contemporary, unfolding, and unanticipatedly related phenomena:

First, the discoveries of the Americas

Second, the religious reformation

Third, the intent by a mere handful of early scholars to change the morals and manners of unworthy feudal and royal leaders in their homeland Scotland

The discoveries of the Americas are a much-told story, but rarely understood then and now—*then*, because of limited literacy and means of communications;

now, because of the overabundance of facts we could know. Certainly, those who heard of the new lands would expect eventual claims for their governance. Thankfully, the existence of the lands—the New World—came to be, and the vast majority of its area, particularly on the north continent, did mostly lie fallow politically* for much of the next two centuries.

It is worth lingering here for a few paragraphs—relevant to our central message—to expand on a little-told story about how the continents' name came to be.

Amerigo Vespucci was a contemporary of Columbus and often referenced in our history textbooks in school. He was a young man of means, a broad-gauged student interested in profound subjects like cosmography and astronomy, engaged by the Medicis of Florence to pursue their interest in Spain and Portugal, and became an outfitter of ships there.

On his own initiative first, and shortly thereafter the separate and cooperative interests of the Crowns

---

* In the sixteenth century, what governance there was came from the traditional native tribes and from a few Spanish settlements. In the seventeenth century, flocks of Dutch, Swedes, Germans, and Finns appeared, joined by broader settlements of the French and then predominately the spread of English colonies.

of Spain and Portugal, he explored expansively the shore and some lands south of Columbus's discovery of the "Indies"—the Caribbean region was early on so defined. His extensive coastline observations and prolific picturesque reports were the subject of a nebulous printed French letter entitled "Mundus Novus," penned by Vespucci describing his four voyages between 1497 and 1504.

At the same time, an obscure clergyman by the name of Martin Waldseemüller became canon of the monastery in the duchy of Lorraine, France. The ruling duke and wealthy supporters aspired to cultivate the arts and engaged the monks.

Waldseemüller and his colleagues hoped to print a new edition of Ptolemy's geography, but when they learned the content of the four voyages, they alertly produced a different volume called *Cosmographiae introductio,* describing what to them was a new fourth part of the world. Europe, Africa, and Asia were then known to Ptolemy. Waldseemüller, who fancied himself a master of names, did write, "In as much as both Europe and Asia received their names from women, I see no reason why anyone should justly object to calling this fourth part Amerige,"* which translated into the

---

* From the Greek "ge" meaning "land of." Daniel J. Boorstin, *The Discoverers,* p. 253

land of America. It is well documented that the great sailor-adventurer made no hint or suggestion to the use of his name.

In company of the new volumes, a map, grand in size and detail, with dominating portraits of Ptolemaeus and Vespucius, was also published and circulated. The full title of the map is "Universales cosmagraphia secunda Ptholemei traditionem et Americi Vespucci aliorum que lustrationes" (a drawing of the whole earth following the tradition of Ptolemy and the travels of Amerigo Vespucci and others). An original and only remaining copy now hangs prominently in the Library of Congress.

Ironically, Waldseemüller did shortly change his mind about crediting Amerigo Vespucci as the true discoverer. But it was too late to persuade a retraction. The map and volumes were circulated in influential places. He had applied the name primarily to the southern region, but when Johannes Schoner in 1515 and Peter Apian in 1520 adopted the name and Gerardus Mercator published his widely acclaimed map of the world in 1538, a South America and a North America were confirmed. A stage was named that was to become the site for the eventual emergence of the wisdom of our Founding Fathers.

Panel of 1507 world map by Martin
Waldseemüller showing America in the
inset and the illustration of Vespucius.

Panel of 1507 world map
by Martin Waldseemüller
showing the name "America"
in the continent.

Scottish History from
AD 1500

All wisdom must have roots. Theirs (the founders) was to derive in critical part from the spectacular, unscripted set of not anticipatable stirrings of men's bodies and souls and minds in Europe, and particularly Scotland, through the next centuries. We know today that such stirrings, which may at times seem less sure of purpose or even bordering on the chaotic, have an eventual quality of self-organizing for some good, and often for the greater good. It is such a set of events we now will explore, which did evolve for our greater good.

The Scotland we have come to know was a melding of fierce tribes whose members survived a just-bearable, hardened life imbuing a steadfastness that molded a try-to and to-do character. Over the generations, it so achieved its nascent character at least the equal of the better-developing European societies leading up to the midmillennium.

It's land was settled by Iberians, Celts, and Picts*
before the Christian era. The Romans conquered it in
AD 80. They named it Caledonia. A different tribe of
Celts called Scottish from Ireland established a colony
on Caledonia's west coast about AD 500, changed
the name, and by force and persuasion converted the
largest part of the population to Christianity.

The uniting of the tribes into the first kingdom, AD
844, followed many painful struggles, but some order
did follow, including the chartering of towns and a
parliament. During the Norman conquest of England,
1066, many English refugees fled to Scotland. Some
received land grants and promoted feudalism.

In the early thirteenth century, trade and social
qualities improved, and there was an actual peace with
England for almost one hundred years—a welcome
contrast to the past, but not to last.

The assertion of sovereign leadership over the country
by natives and then the English monarchy and then
again the local authorities was repeated almost
endlessly for the next centuries. The English Crown
would declare its sovereignty and take to battle. The
Scottish, who now had their own aristocracy, just
as readily declared their independence and flexed

---

* A people who painted themselves.

their armament with France, England's nemesis, in the wings.

The teachings of the churches had become critically contentious. By the mid fifteenth century, the Roman Catholic Church was the official church of Scotland. Many Scottish were resentful, particularly of the apparent imperial intent of the papacy. Contests abounded. By 1560, the Scottish parliament led by the vigorous John Knox caused the parliament to establish the Presbyterian Church as the national church. But beliefs continued diversely in abounding ways, which will cause us to return to greater effects of the reformations of religions in due course.

These selected history highlights provide a bare sketch of the energetic ebb and flow toward establishing Scottish nationhood as the millennium entered its second half for a people in dire want.

The most sorrowful of wants was hope—its absence. The majority of the people were subject to repressive control of various pockets of power, obliged to helplessly witness indulgent acts and corruptions of an enlarging "lordly" crowd. Many local civic leaders, princes, and monarchs were unprincipled in their governance as well as scandalous and/or indolent in their public/personal conduct. That crowd, also made up of many of the feudal lords and some of those who contrived virtual baronies and various levels of the aristocracies, were undisguisedly motivated by personal advantage and pleasure without adequate regard for the decent needs of the part of the mass of the population they were purporting to lead.

Although Scotland was as literate and sprinkled with distinguished scholarship at the time as other nations of the European region, the multitude of the people were not offered useful means of self-improvement, and thus could not figure out for themselves what to do about their plight.

Most must have been so busy bleakly keeping up with the universal wants of feeding, clothing, shelter, and caring as best they could for the health of their family while serving their master that their hope for a right or some freedom or relief from the conditions they faced would have been suppressed. Yet, even in those days and in that place, man's higher instinct to control one's own destiny was innate, just dormant. It was capable of being awakened.

Alas, alongside those less fortunate were other Scottish who had risen in the ranks of an ever-coalescing class of the literate and scholarly. A few of these deeply cared and would dare.

One can only imagine that any small handful of the educated thinkers, when initially contemplating the clearing of this confounding maze, would themselves have to overcome a feeling of virtual futility and helplessness. They did overcome by simply *daring to start to do something*—actually something profound—about the plight of their fellows and the leadership of their country.

Those Who Dared and Cared

From among a moderate-sized community* of Scottish historians, two emerged, and, together with a thinker-in-common from Paris, began to pen themes in the early 1500s somewhat similar to each other, raising concern about the imposed-upon conditions of Scottish body politic, with an intent to rectify the causes.

The three were

Hector Boece, who, during a part of the years of his initial influence, was principal of Kings College.

John Major (Mair), an in-residence French scholar whose thinking and published essays had parallels to Boece's and whose expanded Common Sense

---

* By 1500, Scotland had three quality universities.

thesis survived into the influential eighteenth-century Enlightenment period.

George Buchanan, early on and for generations, was acknowledged by his many supporters and detractors alike as the scholar of scholars in his field. His thinking challenged entrenched ways and officials. Other historians and the many-privileged citizenry challenged him. But like the other two of similar mind he dared to advocate bold new principles.

Three principal and sophisticated examples of their fundamental calls to action are the following:

In 1526, Hector Boece wrote his *Scotorum historiae* with major emphasis on morals and the need for their ascendant application in a society where man would have a chance to do better for himself and others in the humanist mode.

In 1521, John Major published *Historia majoris Britanniae* that portrayed an elective social way of life for individuals.

In that period, George Buchanan had completed his history of Scotland that was a highly sought reference for generations. A compelling illustration of his wisdom is best captured in an extract from

*Virtue, Learning and the Scottish Enlightenment,** written by David Allan of the University of Edinburgh cited here:

But most admired and most reviled was always to be the disturbingly radical turn to Buchanan's humanism. His frank indebtedness to the political philosophy of Cicero and the Stoics produced a distinctive theory of government, which was singularly to reverberate through the work of successive venerations of Scottish historians.

Buchanan's dangerous political cutting-edge was in fact achieved by the misleadingly simple device of locating the origins of human society within a fundamentally historical context. By this means he was able to deny in De jure regni apud Scotos (1579) that passive obedience to the constituted political authorities had ever been a natural obligation on the subject. Buchanan argued, in a conjectural history of society borrowed from Cicero, that there had actually been a historical time, when 'men did dwell in cottages, yea and in caves, and as strangers did wander to and fro without Lawes, or certain dwelling places'. It seemed certain to

---

* David Allan, *Virtue, Learning and the Scottish Enlightenment* (Edinburgh: Edinburgh University Press, 1993), 33-34.

Buchanan, in fact, that political society itself had emerged within the bounds of historical time when men 'did Assemble together as their fond humours did lead them, or as some comodity and comon utility did allure them'. If political organisation was thus the product of previous human decisions, Buchanan continued, then it could not rightly be said to be of divine ordination. And if this was so, then government owed its very legitimacy to the fallible preferences of individual men. Buchanan now found himself with only one conclusion available: 'the people have the power to conferre the Government', he proclaimed, 'on whom they please'. Men, it was clear, and even when acting as individuals—the individuals from whom society had first been formed—were sovereign. Indeed, they might actually have an obligation for their own self interests, and have no regard to the publick utility'. These carefully-worded principles were of course enunciated in a kingdom already struggling painfully with the political legacy of Mary's deposition, as well as with a monarchy that in any case had always been congenitally unstable?

Note Buchanan's elegant language:

- "assemble as fond humors did lead them"
- "or some common utility did allure them"
- "not of divine ordination"

- "government owed its legitimacy to the *fallible* preferences of individual men"

These are simple truths. Together they make for profound wisdom. Is it any wonder that a grand Enlightenment might evolve should more such thinking prevail?

And more such thinking did prevail from the literati, of course. And a plodding parade of learned citizens who did steadily swell the ranks of the outspoken. With each generation, new intellectuals would emerge from the ranks, spicing the messages of the masses. It was as if there could be a strengthening set of force fields with a latent magnetism of thinkers begetting thinkers.

The quest for the bettering of leadership was in motion. Hope could and would bud.

Ironically, the quest added to the historical unrest and the motion to the unending commotion in this land in constant ferment. This counterproductive cultural/societal environment challenged the pace of inevitable improvements.

We have limited ourselves to the briefest litany of the country's inherent pre-seventeenth-century fermenting obstacles summarized here:

The ignoble conduct of leaders
The concurrent suppression of individual rights
The revolving wars with England
The citizens' obligation and privilege, therein, to
    take up arms
Limited available education, early on
An economy bare of opportunity to the populace
All of which in concert were discordant, disordering,
    and disheartening—a land in ferment into the
    next century.

Introduction
to Reforms in Religion

But a provocation as tumultuous as any of the others was the reform in religion. The Reformation was as dynamic and transformational in Scotland as anywhere. Fortunately, every religious preachment carried some uplifting moral message.

The Reformation raised profound questions of principle and bias. Questions were often deeply personal and were ever institutionally destabilizing. Each soul and each church were forced to scramble, in varied ways:

- Some in defiance of Catholicism and the pope
- Some puzzled by over proliferation of Protestant claims
- Some retreated to Episcopalian resistance

And on through an almost endless list of what to many of the faithful were heresies breeding acrimony and leading even to martyrdom.

Is it any wonder that such consequences occurred when God's role relating to the nature of man and his societal association was debated? These were inseparable from others—"divine mysteries" and the ageless political assumption of the divine right of monarchs.

Calvinism led the way. Above all, its teachings and convictions caused stress on church and state and citizens with unsettling consequences while winning converts.

Early on, John Knox's roles were extraordinary and effective as he and others preached the doctrine of predestination—predetermination of each life by the omniscient and omnipotent God. That doctrine asserted that man could not by himself intend a significant objective and fulfill it himself. Yet the creed took sections of the faithful by storm. The mobility of many members, among the Kirks, was close to seismic. Many were attracted to the reactionary belief while others repelled to more comfortable choices.

Ironically, no church was comforting, because the universal gospel from most denominational pulpits was "Fear the wrath of God!" Each neighboring cleric seemed to preach fear more graphically than the next.

At this point in our study, we interject a relevant digression. The brevity of attention offered here about the Religious Reformation risks a disservice because it is such an all-encompassing subject unto itself. We have to be selective when intending to emphasize critical interdependent factors that fuse with the "founder" message of this book.

Certain relevant factors were:

- Did the Reformation contribute to the ferment in Scotland that helped breed its advancing scholarship?

It did. To begin with, most of the Scottish had a naturally acquired acceptance of devotion to a God, but church choices covered a spectrum of competing Christian dogmas. Each major competing religion avowed its own schooling, its sermons from the pulpits and its influencing of higher vocations at the college level to strengthen its faith and membership. Beneficially, religious studies complemented non-theological educational intents often.

- How did it challenge the confidence that humanist thinkers could have in forwarding their noble morals and manners intents?

Recall that the principle of humanism was a belief in God as the "father" who engrained in man natural, intellectual, and other resources with which man could develop and electively do things to better himself. The Calvinist principle of predetermination/predestination denied the existence of such natural human resources and achievements. The humanist school of thinking dominated in the sixteen century. The humanist school sustained itself more than well enough in the seventeenth and a good part of the eighteenth; although acceptance of predeterminism was on an accelerated rise, not enough to mute the progressive thinkers in the time of our ongoing story.

- How did its energies eventually act as the carrier of secular wisdom to the North American colonists?

Well before the mid 1700s, an increasing number of Scottish of all persuasions and professions—those of the least standing and talents as well as the better among the whole—were emigrating to the colonies. A healthy cadre of those who had risen through the universities into the ministries (comparatively, a generous percentage of them were Episcopalians) was settling in the Chesapeake areas. More often than not, these ministry and other leader types had acquired/absorbed significant scholarship in other vital subjects applicable to differing useful ends.

In the spirit of acknowledging the Reformation breadth, we additionally herald here three of its enduring initiators and spokesmen whose beliefs spread to Scotland:

Erasmus, 1466-1536, Dutch, he was his own apostle of moderation and Christian humanism.

Luther, 1483-1546, German, the advocate of "justification by faith."

Calvin, 1509-1564, French, moved on to Switzerland, an eminent ecclesiastical organizer otherwise featured in this text.

All of them in one way or another espoused democratic governance within their church, but were at odds as to the ways to seek salvation. Their differences and dissensions, in spite of lofty dogmas and eventual harmony, played out discordantly for many decades.

Scotland's Growing Strength

The influence of the role of historiography for Scotland was increasingly consequential throughout the two emergent centuries, sixteenth and seventeenth. It reflected the Scottish inbred disposition. To them, history was a great teacher. Writing history was the even better teacher. The history writer desired to be read and understood and be influential. Those who followed our three vanguard challengers for better leadership also confidently took on that audience of unworthy leaders. They built on their collective background of learning through history.

Some of the earlier of the Scottish historians had an in-depth attraction to the Greeks and Romans. Latin and Greek were the vernacular. Many hoped they could distill solutions from those many ancient accounts that could relieve some current travail. A cadre of them dared to wonder if a proliferation of the Mediterranean philosophies and practices from Plato, Aristotle,

Socrates, et al., could be implanted and refined to make of Edinburgh and Glasgow the "Athens of the North." That was an overreach, of course, but was an intent to be proud of. Others were assiduous students of the continent's Renaissance writers.

It was generally understood that it was the practice and mission of the history writers of those much earlier eras to just perpetuate heritages. To delve deep or overly interpret was uncommon. The ranks of our Scottish history authors were not so shy. They were expanding in numbers and were expansive as advocates of interpretations of their instructive lessons.

Many leaders, and much of the populace, were now taking heed of virtue and disciplined conduct along with more acts of unselfish public service. A unique consequence of that latter public spirit was a firm and final movement to a citizen-staffed military in place of the traditionally mercenary forces partially employed. It was as if to say, "This is my country, which I now respect more, should I not fully defend it personally?"

These were good happenings. But the issue of sovereignty was not as easily resolved by persuasion. The intrigues of the courts—the English in London, the Scottish in Edinburgh—the accidents of life of monarchs, and the behind-the-scene maneuvers by special interest traders and power brokers contrived to unite the Crowns in 1603 with a significant shift of influence to the south. The Scottish parliament and judiciary remained at home.

The loss of the Crown was a blow not easily absorbed. It was an on going irritant throughout the century with recurring militancy, but it did not deter continuing, though halting, progress of a Scotland dedicated to bettering itself. Scotland was evolving a unique combination of cultures and customs, including the following:

1. An emphasis was set on general education. This view was supported by a high interest (for its time) in education unto itself. It was now possible, and the time for ordinary men to become better educated and join a chorus for virtue rather than just the privileged obtaining an education. The English, incidentally, favored a specialized education.

2. A dual disposition by many was characterized by a strong will to speak out that was paradoxically matched by a healthy quotient of tolerance for others to be heard (not necessarily with agreement but tolerated).

Through these formative two and a half centuries, general tolerance in Scotland was allegedly greater than in some foreign arenas and was frequently cited as being so in the eighteenth century in spite of ongoing vitriolic theological disagreements.

3. The thinking citizens had that natural inclination to write history! Even the emergent author could observe what was taking place around him, such as the low life of a prince, the injustice of a lord, or an inspiring service to the kirk. To write the evidence of conditions and possibilities was encouraged and respected.

The country was setting national qualities unparalleled elsewhere. These included

- the most hospitable and stimulating environment for scholarship;
- a well-developed aggregation of open-minded universities;
- the maturing of knowledge in most topics that promised *accelerated learning and its application;*
- a history of virtually breeding more and better scholars who relayed their talents to generational successors over almost three centuries;

- a captivating *momentum that seemed to refuel* itself.

Science and law were just two of many applicable fields of knowledge where the Scottish were achieving to higher measures. The seventeenth century was notable at home and abroad for discoveries in physics, mathematics and medicine. From abroad they did readily absorb

- the philosophy and mathematics of Rene Descartes (1596-1650) and
- the physics and mathematics of Isaac Newton (1642-1727).

At home, they had

- The influence and leverage of the founder of a "family dynasty in science," James Gregory (1638-1675), a friend of Newton's, inventor of the reflecting telescope, first professor of mathematics at the University of Edinburgh. His sons and grandsons followed in his footsteps, filling leading positions as professor of medicine at King College, the medical chair at Edinburgh, and many others.
- David Gregory, a nephew of James Gregory (1661-1708), a distinguished astronomer who from 1683 to 1691 was professor of mathematics

at the University of Edinburgh, where he taught the theories of Newton prior to their being offered in England. The Gregory circles were awesome.

- Sir Robert Sibbald (1641-1722), who played an integral role in Edinburgh's prominence in medicine. Sibbald studied on the continent, as did some other scholars, and brought his skills back to Scottish centers. He was joined by notable contemporary colleagues such as James Halket and Archibald Petcairne.

These individuals as well as significant others ensured that the rest of the world of medicine and science and scholars in general could not ignore Scottish thinking.

The sophistication of the law was evolving in many countries, and Scotland was motivated to keep up. Sir James Dalrymple (later Viscount Stair, 1616-1695) and Sir George Mackenzie (1636-1691) were senior leaders and teachers. Stair was expert in civil law; Mackenzie was renowned in criminal law. They were able teachers and practitioners who honorably borrowed unashamedly from top legal minds on the continent, such as Samuel Pufendorf, whose teaching also influenced Francis Hutcheson (who virtually launched the Scottish Enlightenment). But even their best efforts left an opening for their successors to blend

ROBERT W. GALVIN

and upgrade advanced theses of social theory, politics, ethics, and rhetoric into a strong case for Scotland to stand eventually as a peer to other nations "before the bar."

The national "curricula" of the searching minds now included

religion	law
historiography	science
social theory and politics	human nature
economics	aesthetics
ethics	

with their myriad of subtopics.

A remaining topic was uniquely significant—rhetoric. Early language pronunciations and grammar challenged understandability and persuasiveness. As we meet the principal scholars of the Enlightenment, we will discover that certain of them are looked up to in a scholastic role as rhetorician along with their other honors. The language skills they imparted were keys to the Scottish communications excellence. Incidentally, oratory was a favored therapy as well as an often-used speaking technique.

The initiatives of those few Scottish decades and decades ago (early 1500s) to give hope to their countrymen in dire want sparked the engraining of these fundamentals far beyond any early expectation. This extraordinary achievement prepared Scotland to deal not only with its recurring, stinging, transitory events but prepared it for the unparalleled challenge of its combined theological, political, legal, human nature, moral philosophy puzzle, which sought the better way of life. Scotland was proving to be the compelling setting for the finest minds to engage.

And those fundamentals provided it with the strength and resilience to absorb the troubles that would yet mark the transition out of the seventeenth century.

A few years before, influential national leaders in government and in private sector roles persuaded themselves and a now-existent wealthy class that the country must have colonies on the North American continent to stand up to England. The strategy was called the Darien scheme (a fateful name). Its selection of and plans and execution of a Central American settlement was tragic in cost of people's lives and the loss to the treasury—the government's as well as the citizens'. The consequences threatened bankruptcies.

Not long thereafter, like the shenanigans that cost the country its Crown in 1603, in 1707 the trade-off of conflicting political and economic interests bargained away the parliament. Now administrative, legislative and some judicial powers were to be centered in London.

These back-to-back calamities cast another pall. Spirits were dulled, of course. The conditions of earning a living were further retarded early on by the sapping degrees of confidence within those who might commit the next levels of business-enhancing investments. The try-to and to-do character was challenged again. Its most immediate, hopeful sign was the beginning increment of better trading opportunities to the south, to the factions who welcomed a united kingdom.

The last of the "stinging transitory events" to which we allude are the unsettling and unpromising pseudorevolutions of 1715 and 1745. The longing for independence would simmer on but finally ebb.

The ferment we have trod and now leave behind was obviously unsettling. Ferment in its essence is a process of nature. Nature has a way of bringing its processes in balance—though not always immediate or immediately obvious. Over this next short stretch of time, the early 1700s, the next generation of thinker-citizens who would be the successors of the earlier progressive activists who had borne that centuries-long unsettling heat would arrive on the scene. They too would be fermenters, seemingly imbued with a healthful yeast that would stir theirs and other men's minds to the utmost for the greater good.

The stage was being set for the casting of the Scottish Enlightenment. Learned men, one scholar after another, would begin to speak up and to their enthusiastic surprise find themselves joining in the most stimulating intellectual assembly in history.

The Casting of the Scottish Enlightenment

On the first page of this book, the Scottish Enlightenment was described. For ease of reference that is restated here.

The Scottish Enlightenment was about to be

- the grandest aggregation for any given time in history of the leading scholars from virtually *all* then-existing fields of knowledge,
- thinking together in one locale,
- during a single compressed era of time—a decade or two before and after 1750.

What was left unsaid was the definition of *enlightenment*. A dictionary states, "A philosophical movement in European countries that emphasized rationalism, intellectual freedom, and freedom from prejudice and superstition in social and political activity."

It is important to recall that in the Middle Ages, and lingering up to the eighteenth century, the social, political, *and religious* dialogues were replete with (1) myth and superstition, (2) prejudice in favor of *who* had pronounced a belief versus *what* might be provable as true, and (3) intolerance of even the expressions of others. These were societies of all too many closed minds.

Our early role model Scottish were gifted with an enlightened instinct, not only asserting the freedom to say what one would say, but an active willingness to do so. They came to understand that enlightened thinking was *the way of thinking*—free, tolerant, objective, and to the best of one's ability, rational but not dependent on assured, initial correctness, though what you thought and expressed was important, of course. The open questioning of those thoughts and expressions held the promise of the better, realistic conclusions. To top it off, they added the elixir of a place for high morals and manners.

Let's begin our acquaintanceship with the great men. In fact, most readers already know of at least the first named scholars and appreciate their excellence.

The following list introduces the core of the whole, each equivalently brilliant and incomparably influential individually and as a group:

James Watt

The Author of the Wealth of Nations

Adam Smith

James Watt, who vastly improved the steam engine

Robert and James Adams, architects, bridge builders, and town planners

Adam Smith, author of *An Inquiry into the Nature and Causes of the Wealth of Nations* and *The Theory of Moral Sentiments*; interrelated economic behavior, jurisprudence, engineering, cities, even astronomy

Francis Hutcheson, moral philosopher; author: "The Right to Resistance"; credited with lighting the Enlightenment

David Hume, economic philosopher; focused on first causes, nature of morality, miracles and religion, history, liberty and political authority; a practical skeptic

James Hutton, founder of modern geology, which leads to the understanding of plate tectonics and the ages-long formation of the earth

Joseph Black, father of modern chemistry, who fathomed latent heat; a physician and consultant to industry

Hugh Blair, rhetorician and literary language scholar; distinguished cleric, historical sermons

James Burnett (Lord Monboddo), anthropologist, philosopher, judge, and founder of modern historical linguistics

Henry Horne (Lord Kames), who related legal, philosophical, and literary inquiries with political experiments in agriculture; personally gave John Adams a copy of his *Historical Law Tracts*

Dugald Stewart, philosopher, economist, and teacher; historian of the Enlightenment

Thomas Reid, advocate of the more "common sense" understanding of often complex issues

Adam Ferguson, founder of sociology; author: *History of Civil Society*

William Robertson, one of the founders of modern historiography, a major study of feudalism

William Cullen, master chemist and medical researcher; a "master" in business as well.

John Millar, who integrated the subjects of law, social structure, rhetoric, and philosophy

David Hume

Francis Hutcheson

These were complemented by a score or more of colleagues of highest merit like Sir John Sinclair, Sir James Stewart, John Erskine, George Campbell, and others deserving of the laudatory reviews by many of today's students of eighteenth-century Scottish history. These colleagues' thinking integrated with the core and enhanced it.

A pleasing coincidence played in their favor. Most of the men of the Enlightenment were born at about the same time. They virtually grew wise together mostly in Edinburgh and Glasgow. About three-quarters were born between 1710 and 1725 and reached their prime just about our pivotal time, circa 1750. From then on their works only brightened.

Only two of the principals, Francis Hutcheson and Lord Kames, started life as early as the 1690s. Both were young of mind, and Lord Kames was highly productive through the prime of life of the others. Dugald Stewart was not born until 1753, so his influence for the benefit of the Founding Fathers was to be limited. His was the privilege of looking over the shoulder of the movement. By looking back from the turn of the century, his reviews helped to immortalize the Enlightenment.

It was he who is purported to have answered the question, where did it come from? with another question, was it born of a "sudden burst of genius?" He knew better, of course, but his invoking the dynamic term, burst, played into my natural proclivity, counter-intuition:

- It was not a single burst
- It was stronger than a burst
- It was the opposite of a burst
- It was the genius of a people who had the patience and the fortitude over centuries to allow their recipe for betterment to ripen to fruition.

Our patience is rewarded by appreciating that the Scottish Enlightenment revealed itself for what it had begun to be and would become around our "central" date, 1750. That timing is not at odds with the Enlightenments on the continent. The Enlightenment thinkers in both places had to mature and earn recognition and acceptance.

It fascinates me to reflect on my schooling that did feature the subject of an enlightenment, but it was all continental. There was merit in my learning from Montesquieu (1689-1755), Voltaire (1694-1778), and Rousseau (1712-1778), all of them from France, Kant of Germany (1724-1804) and a few other greats. But as significant as were their messages, they were few in the numbers of authors, limited in spectrum of subjects, and scattered among countries. Scotland's became an "Enlightenment Universale."

It is not out of order to credit Francis Hutcheson's publication of a distinguished treatise in 1725 with lighting the Scottish way. This was his *An Inquiry into the Original of Our Ideas of Beauty and Virtue*. Beauty, as he uses the term, is the outward form of things that reflects inward qualities. His focus dealt with all that mankind, possessing a natural internal sense of beauty, should strive to countenance about nature's tangible aesthetics and virtue; how mankind, possessing a cultivatable moral sense, should aspire to unselfishly deserve approbation for one's benevolence *contributing to* personal good and *the "public good."*

The treatise—in fact there are two in series—set a profound standard of scholastic quality and integration of ideas, cerebrally challenging an enlightenment stage setting. Franklin, Adams, and Jefferson were three colonials among others who referenced it seriously.

As we will account, numerous practical governance lessons were to flow to our founders even if the title of the opening treatise may not have signaled its actual utility. This broad thinker, Hutcheson, could not have been additionally more relevant to what colonists should eventually think than his unparalleled free-standing essay "The Right to Resistance", the essence of which incidentally was introduced in the second of the *Original* treatises. It is the opinion of many authorities that the "Resistance" essay is the most thorough, reasonable, persuasive, and thus influential of all such advocacies then in circulation. Yes, there were others, but his was better and prominent in Scotland—a land perpetually resisting. It was to be a favored reference in many of the thirteen colonies. Regrettably, he died in 1746 and was never to know his influence on the many whose courage to resist had to be strengthened a score of years later and whose language and spirit of expression was to serve Thomas Jefferson ten years beyond.

This being the first example alleging a useful influence on colonists, let's establish a principle that should be interpreted into the other beneficiaries as well.

A basic lesson of life is one wins at the margin. If those of us of equal skill would race, one would win but only by a short step. Put another way, increments make a difference. Winning by that increment makes a big difference. All of the factors of benefit we will cite will be important, but few were exclusive to the Scottish. Some of the Scottish lessons were more timely. Some more bold. Some more complete. Each more persuasive to selected individual patriots and often to many of them. In the aggregate, the Scottish Enlightenment's lessons imparted a margin: an increment of wisdom that made our founders' founding the winner among all the founding in history.

Scottish penny commemorating Adam
Smith,
1723-1790, by P. Kempson

Scottish penny commemorating Adam
Smith,
1723-1790, by P. Kempson

Our Guiding Questions

How can we refine our understanding? By delving into the answers to these questions:

First, how did the maturing sages conduct themselves to heighten their given scholarship?

Second, what were the insights and principles that their individual and/or interactive thinking surfaced for the use of our founders?

Third, how were these ideas conveyed to and embraced by the influential in North America?

Fourth, how did the U.S. founders synthesize what they learned with that which they ably conceived and formulated themselves?

Let's proceed.

First, how did the maturing sages conduct themselves to heighten their given scholarship?

- They thought the way of Enlightenment: free, tolerant, objective, and rational.
- As able students, they gained from the country's superior schools and university system.
- They taught—a no better way to learn more.
- They lectured, delivering many and listening as well.
- Sermons: Hugh Blair's venue was the pulpit. His sermons, theologically centered, ranged over virtually all tantalizing issues. Published as a collection, they are an all-encompassing history of his and colleagues' thoughts.
- The religious disagreements were inescapably distracting, but at the same time these sharpened minds and led to broadened thinking beyond theology.
- They published early and throughout their careers.
- They traveled among the lively domestic communities of Edinburgh, Glasgow, and Aberdeen and the continent. David Hume resided and worked for the Scottish government in Paris, assumed assignments in Vienna and Turin and Holland. Adam Smith tutored a young student on an extended continental tour with

long residence in France. This was not an insular cadre.

- The Clubs! The sages liked people, including, of course, their own kind. They formed clubs so as to gather, often to frolic, and discourse. While sipping a wine and puffing a pipe, propositions, advocacies, an early text, a contestable issue would energize an agenda. These subject matters would echo throughout the community for days. Knowledge and opinions were shared with all in a now mostly literate society. There were many clubs:

The Mirror Club	The Pious Club
The Rankenian Club	The Oyster Club
The Boar Club	The Literary Society
The Cape Club	The Select Society

The Poker Club, not cards, rather provocation
The Philosophical Society in Edinburgh
    became the Royal Society.
And more.

Most of the great men were members of two or three clubs. Interrelations and interdisciplinary thinking knew few bounds.

- They critiqued; they challenged "old truths." Adam Smith criticized English commercial-economic ways to the evident displeasure of neighbors to the south. James Hutton was closing in on the forming of the earth and its natural makeup to the distress of theologians' assumptions.

- They believed in themselves.

The Colledge of Glasgow, c. 1693

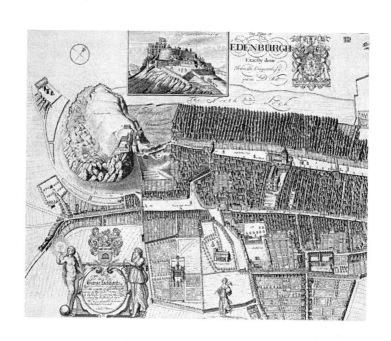

Plan of Edinburgh, c. 1710

Second, what were the insights and principles that their individual and/or interactive thinking surfaced for the use of our founders?

- Morals: Moral philosophy was an up-front centerpiece at Scottish universities. It was to prove to be virtually transplantable.
- Resistance: Most colonists were satisfied to be English citizens and subjects of the King prior to the mid-1770s. Many had to be persuaded as to the right to resist even after the Tea Party and Stamp Act.
  As articulate as our leaders were, they had to learn persuasive tones and spirit of expressing that right to resist. Jefferson, as we will note, was responsive.
- Government structure: David Hume was as much an accomplished political scientist as his other extraordinary expertise. He wrote a collection of essays in 1752 including one on the "Idea of a Perfect Commonwealth." Our delegates to the Constitutional Convention will pay heed.
- A supreme role for commerce. Earnable wealth is essential to affording a freedom-sustaining government. Financial means allow for launching a new country without the larceny of piracy and plunder. Jay G. Prokop, a scholar of scholars, attested,

o The great achievement of the Scottish school of sociological historians was the recognition that a commercial organization of society had rendered obsolete much that had been believed about society before.

- The role of virtue in and for commerce and the role of commerce in fostering virtue was a genuine advocacy.
- They generated a newly understood role of property—the sinew of not only the businesses of commerce but honorably held personal possessions. Dr. David Allan, author of *Virtue, Learning and the Scottish Enlightenment*, lauded this fundamental and expressed it in a relevant historical context.

o The history of property, which characterized the historical scholarship of eighteenth century Scotland, may thus be understood only as a special case in a long cultural continuum. It was enhanced by contemporary economic and intellectual trends, but was consistent still with the slowly evolving Scottish exploration of morality and manners begun by Hector Boece.

The vital and complex role of property was simplified by its common sense depiction at each stage of society's evolution:

- Hunter-gatherers consumed their edible daily.
- Herders' possessions were almost constantly on the move.
- Farmers settled on land, used tools, and held inventory.
- Commercial ownerships were more complicated.

The more detail minded thought through various sizing and mixings of property, including inventory, which raised the competence of those who would manage.

- Common sense: While it is likely that every generation of mankind aspired to common sense and some probably believed they were masters, the Enlightenment principals searched out the subject more profoundly. Our able founders had proper and natural inclinations, no doubt, but those who would read Thomas Reid could better bring a simple clarity to a complex subject.
- The Lockean thesis: Including Locke's principles among the Scottish Enlightenment is technically incorrect. He lived almost a hundred years earlier and was English. For shame! Locke's ideas of government are contained in and between the lines of the Scottish author's, commanding our attention in this book. They did not disguise their inclusion of this or any other best idea that came their way. Of course, some of Locke's

THE GENIUS OF A PEOPLE

thinking did trace to the insight of that early inspiration, George Buchanan.

Third, how were these ideas conveyed to and embraced by those that were influential in North America?

The Scottish searched within and outside to better their way of life. They scanned other states for lessons to be learned. The colonies had naturally attracted their attention. This was particularly so after the period of benign neglect by the King and the Parliament (the decades before the 1750s) was showing signs of stressful relations between London and its North American subjects. Comparisons of stresses were analyzed in hopes of finding common causes and possible relief strategies.

A most uncommon cause surfaced. It offered a possible solution in the all-consuming contests among religious sects from the lowlands to the highlands. Various sects began to imagine the possibility of greater evangelical success in the "overseas province" than a competing creed, which success they surmised could reflect in a stronger following of their particular flock back in Scotland. Favorable reaction by colonists became a principle hope of those who would reform religion at home.

This prompted increased assignments of clerics to colonial projects and residencies. The underlying motive differed in part from the well-known quests for religious freedoms that drove so many others to America's shores. This development turned into a mid-1700s campaign to capture a greater share of the souls *and minds* of men. Who better than the parsons and ministers to lead this charge? As we read up front, many of them had to supplement their income tutoring thus doubling in the welcome role of general teachers.

Year after year, as more of these church-oriented assignments were assumed, these theologians/ teachers or teachers/theologians, who themselves had been the students or audience of the Enlightened became prominent conveyors of the thinking fed by this uncommon enlightened source. A synopsis of Professor T.M. Devine's objective portrayal of the knowledge exchange between the two people follows in a few pages.

The networking conditions among the learned and learning Scottish back home were ideal. Virtually all the educated were in frequent contact with each other in the main communities. Edinburgh and Glasgow for example had populations of about thirty thousand each. Thus, almost everyone could know almost every other body and the enlightening thoughts that flowed freely among them. And so it followed that an "intellectual gospel" could be spread to the colonies.

We also learned at the front of the book that James Madison was tutored. Donald Robertson, a Scottish who had studied at Aberdeen and Edinburgh universities, was one to whom Madison voiced high praise for the schooling Robertson had rendered to him. Francis Allison, a pupil of Hutcheson, came to the colonies in 1735 as a tutor to the Dickenson family of Maryland and later taught at least three signers of the Declaration of Independence. Many youths of the mid-1700s were similarly trained on through secondary education.

One of the more prominent educators from Scotland, if not the most respected, was Rev. John Witherspoon, who became the president of the University of New Jersey at Princeton. One of Madison's professors, he was renowned for his toleration of the more contentious societal views of Hume and Robertson. A conservative by nature, he saw to the balanced exposure of his students to all pre-Enlightenment and Enlightenment thinking. In his autobiography, Edinburgh-educated Dr. Benjamin Rush wrote that Witherspoon "gave a new turn to education" in "taste and correctness. It was easy to distinguish his pupils everywhere whenever they spoke or wrote for the public."

Scottish moral philosophy was an integral part of the curricula of most American colleges of the time. William Small, then at the College of William and

Mary, professor of moral philosophy and rhetoric, read with and taught Thomas Jefferson for his first two university years and carried on a close scholarly association following Jefferson's studies at Princeton, also shaped by Witherspoon. Jefferson later credited Small for much of the success he achieved.

The effects of Scottish thinking were eminent in many ordinary ways and places. For example, when the Continental Congress wanted a list of books available for the use of the Congress, it appointed a committee chaired by James Madison and including John Lowell of Massachusetts and Madison's former mentor, John Witherspoon. The list, submitted in January 1783, included Scottish authors throughout—Hume, Smith, Ferguson, Millar, and others—most of whose books Madison, Witherspoon, and Jefferson also personally owned and studied.

A transcending historic impact was the surfacing of a principle that was to shape a critical fundamental of our emergent free society. It flowed from an integration of newly emphatic and integrated thinking that called for the increased role of commerce in planning for a nation's development and affordability.

At the beginning of this essay, reference was made to this, being a rarely told, even an untold, story of our republic's founding. Of course, many of us know some important parts of that history, including the role of Adam Smith and the Lockean principles that predated Smith's publications.

What is inadequately appreciated is the common thread referenced by many of the leaders of the Enlightenment of the "link between intellectual and economic development." The links in their chain of thinking were frequent and meaty. For example, Smith, Hume, Ferguson, and others analyzed economic history to its essence. They identified and defined the four stages in the development of mankind and social order. These were hunting-gathering, pasturage, farming, and commerce, which played out over a painstakingly long evolution from a lower to a higher standard of living.

It is significant to note again how pervasive Enlightenment thinking and rhetoric became. While president of the United States, James Madison addressed the Agricultural Society of Albemarle, Virginia, and said in context of a broad-ranging speech, "The hunter becoming the herdsman, the latter a follower of the plow, and the last repairing to manufactory or workshops." Others wrote similarly, even inspiringly. Witherspoon's theme was his "linking commerce to piety."

The dynamic of this class of thinking is further illustrated by an effort at reciprocal influence back to Scotland.

William Thom, a close associate of Witherspoon with strong commercial convictions, recommended that the University of Glasgow revise its curriculum, upgrading and featuring commercial training.

It is not as if the Scottish were presuming to have discovered commerce as such. Rather, they conjured a vision or a hope or a dream (really a proposition) that commerce, which had been around for centuries but influenced just a small proportion of a population's way of life, could expand, and for the better.

No longer was commerce to be looked upon with suspicion. Francis Hutcheson argued that the increased standards of living promoted by commerce would stimulate virtuous behavior.

All at one time and all in one place, the enlightened could envision (in fact, they could hardly help but stumble over their combinable phenomenal achievements) increased power from reliable engines, new materials from new chemistry, finer building construction, transportation infrastructure upgrades, better yields from the earth, health benefits, and more. The sciences were coming of a more useful age. Fresh social, economic, and political concepts offered the promise of operational systems that could harmonize all the above to satisfy beneficial and needed useful arts (business) intents.

Scottish scholars were keenly aware that each nation at times, and most nations and empires all of the time, had afforded themselves only by force; and more often than not, they were founded by force. The synonyms for force at the time were plunder and piracy, not exactly an acceptable way of the world. To these scholars, nations had to find a way to be affordable civilly. Agrarian societies (hunting, herding, etc.) held little promise of total fulfillment. So there was a practical realization that commerce had to and could become an equal among equals in the makeup of subsystems of civil and sustaining nations. This concept was to have a dramatic impact on the constitutional intent of the soon-to-be United States of America.

In defending the new constitution then under consideration for adoption in October 1787, Alexander Hamilton wrote,

> It has been frequently remarked that it seems to have been reserved to the people of this country, by their conduct and example, to decide the important question, whether societies of men are really capable or not of establishing good government from reflection and choice, or whether they are forever destined to depend for their political constitutions on accident and force.

John Witherspoon

William Small

By the mid-1770s, the rebels among the colonists hardly needed any more scholarly justification to resist their king. They declared their independence!

This courageous part of the founding story is well known. Yet few of us are familiar with a curious detail: the proliferation of pre-1776 rhetoric, substantially from the pens of Scottish scholars (again, notably Hutcheson) that composed persuasive, documented justifications for oppressed people to assert their independence.

Thomas Jefferson unquestionably deserves high praise for his part in the superbly reasoned, integrated, and phrased Declaration of Independence text. It should simply be noted that sprinkled throughout the Enlightenment essays are multiple paragraphs similar in thought to each other and not so different from Jefferson's.

Jefferson readily acknowledged that his ideas were not original. He drew upon the Scottish and English writings of the earlier advocates not to find new principles or arguments, but to place before mankind the *common sense, tone, and spirit* of the subject. It is interesting to note that Jefferson here refers to "the common sense of the subject." The overall Scottish Enlightenment ideas were known both then and now as the *"common sense" school* of philosophy. Furthermore, Thomas

THE GENIUS OF A PEOPLE

Paine, in drafting his monumental essay advocating independence, intended to title it "Plain Truth." When, however, Scottish-educated Benjamin Rush suggested "Common Sense" instead, Paine readily accepted the change.

One of the few books that addresses the favorable influence of the Scottish is *A Hotbed of Genius: The Scottish Enlightenment, 1730-1790.** The following extract characterizes that role:

> Given the influence of the Scottish Enlightenment on education, an even more interesting question is whether this Scottish bias influenced the climate of opinion that led to the Declaration of Independence in 1776. The intellectual and philosophical sources of the "self-evident" truths and "unalienable rights" of the Declaration of Independence are to be found in theories of natural law and natural rights. To cite works like Harrington's *The Commonwealth of Oceana* (1656), Locke's *Second Treatise on Government* (1689), Montesquieu's *De l'Esprit des lois* (1748) or those of the Scottish philosophers as of paramount importance is to denigrate the native

---

*   Edited by David Daiches, Peter Jones, and Jean Jones
     Specific article by Archie Turnbull
     The Institute for Advanced Studies in Humanities
     University of Edinburgh

convictions of the Americans. However it is possible to argue that the spirit that infuses many of the central doctrines of Congress, from 1774 to 1787, is in peculiar harmony with the legal, philosophical and moral teachings of Hutcheson, Reid, and Kames; whose views in turn reflect the historical and constitutional inheritance of Scotland itself. Directly through their books, and as mediated by their disciples in the American colleges, the ideas of these three men were familiar to all the most eminent statesmen, Franklin, John Adams, Dickinson and Jefferson among them.

Thomas Jefferson

James Madison

Alexander Hamilton

One other and recent exposition and examination of the Scottish Enlightenment is in the book, *Scotland's Empire and the Shaping of the Americas 1600-1815* by T.M. Devine, published in 2005. He is university research professor and director of research at the AHRB Center of Irish and Scottish Studies at the University of Aberdeen. He is heralded by his students, readers, peers and special recognition by the Queen.

I presume to feature brief but pithy extracts from the profound, far ranging Chapter 8, Cultural Relationship and the American Revolution, pp 164-187.

"Enlightenment thought was disseminated as part of the Scottish universities teaching process and so was inevitably exported by university trained Scottish and those returning Americans. (Its) appeal in the colonies was its intrinsic religious and political conservatism."

"Enlightenment in Scotland was not anti-clerical or anti-establishment. The close alliance between the Church of Scotland and men of culture . . . gave to Scottish thought an added element of religions respectability."

"The Scot intellectuals offered . . . a belief in autonomous reason which would enable people to

break out of the inertia of old ideas. There was a sense in their writings of basic optimism for a future."

"Intellectual coteries on both sides of the Atlantic were in regular contact not only through correspondence, but also by exchanging books. It was through these channels that distinguished Americans visited Scotland as guests of the Enlightenment elite. Benjamin Franklin came twice."

"William Smith . . . born near Aberdeen . . . was appointed to the Benjamin Franklin College of Philadelphia to teach logic, rhetoric, ethic and natural philosophy. His reformed curriculum involved a decisive departure from the traditional structure of classical learning and formal philosophy. (It) embraced the sciences of chemistry, natural history and astronomy. This was a seminal development in liberal education which thereafter had both an arts and a science base in the advanced curriculum."

"Like its Scottish sisters, the College of New Jersey drew students from across the colonies and not simply from neighboring districts. Even the occasional black and Native American attended classes. One results was that the College 'became a seminary of statesmen' during the Witherspoon's presidency."

". . . Above all else the Scottish Enlightenment became the dynamic engine for the transoceanic transmission of ideas."

At this point and a few others in the chapter, Professor Devine reins us in with his objective critique. He writes: *"Here . . . we enter a minefield . . . the perennial difficulty of Scottish hype."*

"It is easy to be seduced into the trap of what has been called 'the Burns Supper school of Scottish American historians' which uncritically celebrated in a spirit of chauvinistic triumphalism the great deeds of the Scots who were held to be responsible for all that was best in American development . . . Such works fructify and feed the collective ego of a small nation."

But he balances that with:

"Equally, however, to dilute the impact of Scottish intellectuals and academic traditions during the colonial era would be myopic in the extreme."

Professor Devine is the epitome of objectivity. His cautions balance our insights. I hope my cautionary references* to the sum of the *incremental* benefits

---

* See page 35

imparted by the Scottish Enlightenment to the colonists justify my realistic claim of favorable influence on the United States of America founding.

This brings us to the fourth question: How did the U.S. founders synthesize what they learned with what they conceived and formulated?

After reminding ourselves that their uncompromising intent was to guarantee and sustain freedom, it will help us to appreciate answers to the fourth question by first postulating the essence of *what was to be formulated*. The founders faced the daunting task of writing the rules for their new society.

Society, It's Essence

Society is a grand and dynamic system of people and institutions. It is grand because of its size and complexity and dynamic because it is ever changing among many choices.

A system is typically made up of subsystems. The subsystems of society are elements such as education that trains, military that defends, religion that redeems, and others.

Two of the others at the heart of the "founder" story are business and government. Let us position them.

Business

I define business as that subsystem of society that honorably serves the needs of customers at a profit. When you decode this definition and relate business to the other equally important subsystems, you note that business is the only subpart or agent or institution that generates wealth.

Many subsystems bring unique values to the whole. That is their natural vital role. It does not make one better than others. Business benefits from the contributions of others. Its nature, when honorably and capably operated, is to produce an increase in tangible, transactionable wealth that becomes the principal "currency" to afford government and all the other subsystems that government regulates.

Government

Government applies civic order within the system of people and institutions, variously allowing or disallowing degrees of active pursuits. The early lessons of government came from the Greeks. To them, the chief goal of government was the excellence of people. When Plato spoke of human nature, he meant what human beings could become.

The Greeks' preamble to governance was the view that some authority had to know what goodness was and prescribe it as a duty; from the performance of that duty, a right was earned. Note that in that thesis of governance, a right had to be earned. Now there may be some limited appeal to that concept. However, for centuries it has yielded nothing but lordly tyranny. The lords, who thought themselves the better, sparingly granted rights and privileges to individuals from among the multitude whom they deigned to be less worthy.

Shortly before the Scottish Enlightenment, a philosophy emerged from Thomas, Locke, Montesquieu, and others, and even earlier by George Buchanan. When John Locke spoke of people, he meant what human beings are to begin with—simple creatures of nature bestowed with life, with the right to be free to protect it, to sustain it by their voluntary labor, and to ensure the possession of the fruits of that labor, which require civic order. For this, enlightened thinkers concluded that the chief goal of government should be to protect those rights. Note, rights herein are a *given*!

Our Founding Fathers puzzled over the form of government best suited to that principle and the new country. There was a clear leaning to a republic. The problem was that the only models then available to evaluate were small republics. Our prospective country loomed large. Would a large republic sustain liberties and support itself?

James Madison took up the question on the eve of the Constitutional Convention about to convene in 1787. He was not alone, for this was a subject not overlooked by others. Madison reread Hume. In his 1752 essay "Idea of a Perfect Commonwealth," David Hume outlined a theory that if a large republic could ever be formed, it was the more likely to sustain freedom.

Hume reasoned that people had natural self-interests. Those with similar self-interests would be attracted to each other. These associations he called factions. Multiple factions would emerge within a large population. Various factions would offset others. This recurring phenomenon would prevent the aggregation of an oppressive majority.

This and a prescriptive system of checks and balances would make for a long-living republic with the rights of all manner of minorities optimally and increasingly respected. Madison and his peers were so convinced.

They expressed related thoughts, forthrightly. "Men are not angels," they said. "Desire for personal, selfish advantage is not only something to be tolerated but is a force to be put to work for public good." This opinion was not an endorsement of illicit behavior, but rather a pragmatic acknowledgement of tolerable conduct that they believed would be self-correcting. In fact, somewhat like Witherspoon, who saw shades of piety resident in commerce, some founders hoped that commerce based on freedom of choice would nurture virtue.

An unparalleled historic effect of this profound association of thoughts was that our Founding Fathers were the first founders of a country to grasp the importance of basing a society's governance on a foundation cornerstone of commerce, capital, and a growing economy. This compelling purpose—a special role for business—is too little appreciated.

The philosophers and the founders understood that the pursuit of plenty from self-interest developments is essential to affording a growing republic and its enduring qualities. One of the more evident expressions of intent and providers of thrust to this purpose is ordained in the constitutional provision called the Progress Clause or the Inventors Clause, in Article I, Section 8, of the Constitution. It reads, "the Congress shall have power to promote the progress of science and useful arts by securing for limited times to authors and inventors the exclusive right to their respective writings and discovers."

Think of the first stage of that intent. *Vest power to a congress to promote progress from science and the useful arts—business.*

The progress in sciences by the Enlightenment thinkers and others was well known. Its potential for gainful exploitations through the likes of "manufactory and the workshop" was promising. The latter terms obviously were metaphors for the emerging useful arts and new key processes of our word—business.

Think of elevating a personal right to constitutional stature! *A property right derived from the creative labor of the mind.*

One may not remember or may never have heard that this is the only right—yes, the *only* right—granted by the Constitution. In fact, it is the only place where the word *right* is written in the body of the Constitution.

"What about the Bill of Rights?" you say. Those amendments grant no rights! The popularly named Bill of Rights is composed as a prohibitive or cast in negative terminology. It starts with the words, "Congress shall make no laws" (and here I paraphrase) restricting or abridging freedoms of speech, assembly, or religion that man inalienably always possessed even before having constitutionally instituted a government.

Madison argued that such "Bills need not and should not be a part of a constitution." Political preferences prevailed. So he accommodatingly articulated their inclusion by casting them as a prohibition of interferences in preexisting rights.* Thus,

> *the one and only granting of a right to own the labor of your originality, to practice it as a useful business art, and to cause progress is of singular importance!*

This right espouses more than a patent and copyright system. It bespeaks in part the founders' intention to build the American society on its self-supporting economy and to build that economy importantly on property, particularly the capital of the mind. That freedom and affordability were coexisting intents of our Constitution is overtly declared and inescapably implied.

In the United States, the Constitution is the supreme law. The judiciary is the branch of government with the power to decide and enforce the decision of whether a law enacted by the legislature and approved by the president is constitutional, meaning consistent in all ways with the provisions of and the standing

---

* More than incidentally, by his inclusion of the particular breadth of subjects of what became the first ten amendments and his influence in excluding others, he persuaded the remaining holdouts of ratification, leading to the confirmation of a strengthened Constitution.

interpretation of the Constitution. If it is not, that law is rendered moot by the judiciary.

Were our constitutional authors guided by Scotland to this check and balance or was the principle native born?

A preeminent twentieth century member of the Scottish judiciary, Lord Cameron, recently opined that the early Scottish concept of the hierarchical standing of the judiciary over the legislature in determining the constitutionality of a law might have influenced the approved provision in the U.S. Constitution. He noted that at least up to the Union of 1707, the determinative interpretation within Scotland's legal system rested with the supreme courts of Scotland. Viscount Stair had relevantly observed, "We differ from the English whose statutes of Parliament of whatsoever antiquity remain ever in force until they be repealed."

Think of that legal conundrum. The Parliament stands as its own judge of its virtually unwritten constitution. If the legislated law is ever to be repealed, the Parliament must pass a new law so ordering.

Our founder/constitutional authors are most likely to have known the contrasting provisos between the Scotland pre-1707 and the English system. Or at least because of their frequent dealings with Parliament members, they could not help but know of that institution's conflict of interest.

Taking note of how thorough many of them were in learning other Scottish ways, it is likely that they knew and appreciated the earlier role of the supreme courts of Scotland as well. I opine that to be a likely influence. Our authors rose to the correct hierarchical standing of the judiciary.

So the outreaching propellants of our society that must have seemed like heresies—certainly at least fantasies—to many traditionalists are as follows:

Basic rights are a given.

Personal advantage is a constructive force.

A large republic and its freedoms are sustainably affordable by progress in the useful arts (business) built on science.

Congress has the power to promote that progress.

The singularity of the only constitutionally granted right, which is directed to the essential progress in science and commerce, has extraordinary meaning.

Substantial, intentional, inspirational, and instructional lessons did flow to our founders at influential times.

These were seeded by the

Facts

- There was a Scottish Enlightenment.
- Its grandest assembly of scholars advanced the most knowledge per time and place.
- Scotland and the colonies were similar as "provinces."
- The Scottish targeted religious change here to reform religion at home, which fostered a substantial general education in the colonies.
- Scottish thinking stimulated justifiable resistance (revolution), articulating well-reasoned, well-phrased claims for independence not unlike Jefferson's.
- Using Greek philosophy of governance, rights had to be earned.
- Under Lockean philosophy, rights are a given.
- Only one right is granted in the body of the U.S. Constitution: to the "property of the mind."

And nurtured by

Principles

- A new essential role for commerce in national developments was conceived and emphasized.
- The essence of society is defined.

- Business is the only subsystem of society that generates wealth.
- A large republic breeds factions that mute the tyranny of the majority.
- Self-interest is a force for public good.
- Commerce, capital, and science policies as cornerstone constitutional principles underpin the affordability of a society and the stature of a nation.
- Enlightenment is *the way of thinking*: free, open, objective, rational.
- Mankind's highest aspiration is to control one's destiny. If ever suppressed, it is capable of being awakened.
- We win at the margin. Increments make a real difference.
- Seemingly disjointed dynamic conditions can self-organize for good.
- Confounded? Start to do something!

And made possible by individuals:

Buchanan	The people have the power to confer the government on whom they please.
Hutcheson et al.	The right to resistance The role of virtue
Teachers	Madison, Jefferson, Hamilton, Monroe

from	so tutored by age sixteen
Scotland	William Small's prime influence on Jefferson John Witherspoon, mentor to Madison, Jefferson, and others
Reid Paine Rush	The common sense of "common sense"
Hume	A large republic can best guarantee freedom.
Smith Watt Hutton Black Cullen Adams brothers Millar et al.	Economic and science vitalization available for United States to take advantage
Scottish School of Sociological Historians	The new role for commerce and property in civilly founding and affording a nation

| The Law | Scottish courts' constitutional authority versus statutes of parliament of whatsoever antiquity remaining |

Knowledge of and appreciation of these interrelated facts and basic principles should strengthen our personal enthusiasm and support for our country. The promulgation of these principles to skeptics at home and influential thinkers in other nations can propagate freedom, spawning ground rules for the betterment of the world's continually forming societies.

None of these Enlightenment masters and their many colleagues intended a founding of the United States of America. Yet individually and collectively, their unintended consequence made a giant difference in that most important founding.

Thus, we relearn. Do not underestimate the leverage of the product of scholar-selected scholarship nor demean the power of man to build to a much better life for mankind. Even unintended consequences leave transcending legacies.

Nation Building

On page four of this text, the issue of nation building is introduced. If that subject is one that has kindled your interest at times, it is likely you perceived in this recitation steps toward nationhood with admirable consequences in the eighteenth century.

In spite of its loss of total independence and absorption into the British Empire, Scotland attained and sustained a standing of high admiration and respect unto itself. Its history through the nineteenth and twentieth centuries was consumed with overcoming struggles balanced with major achievements. Regrettably, a next period of Enlightenment was not to be.* But its nationhood quality was and is recognized at home and abroad.

Many of its testimonials are well deserved. One current literary overview that may objectively fill the

---

* Why? If you are curious, please refer to a "A Final Word" role of a surrogate for others that highlight Scotland's fulfillment of its try-to and to-do quality is *How the Scottish Invented the Modern World* authored by Arthur Herman.

I respectfully assert that Scotland is a nation-building role model of merit—as is the United States of America.

What are the principles and guidelines for nation building learned from these two role models, which are as valid today as in the centuries we have just reviewed and as essential tomorrow as before?

- A handful of leaders in the country of promise, thinking along the thought lines that follow, believing in themselves and their high intentions, must step outside the crowd with backbone and advocate what is right. All major change comes from a determination of a minority (Boece and Buchanan/Madison and Jefferson, et al.).
- They plant the seed, which must then be caused to germinate among the roots of the populace. Strength must brew from the bottom. If the handful of leaders were directly forthcoming from that base of the people, all the better.
- The advocacy must be accompanied by a candid acknowledgement of the deficiencies of one's existing country. The key Scottish and colonists

did so. Current lesser-developed nations—leaders and the people alike—are naturally blame placers. To them, their condition is the fault of someone else such as the more successful nations. As long as a country hides behind that invalid excuse, it will languish. Inescapably, the existing deficiencies will be (1) wrong-headed disrespect of freedom and property rights, and (2) an overbearing leadership operating for its selfish ends!

- The reciprocal of that disrespectful and overbearing governance must be the noble purpose of change. Freedom stands first as *the* noble intent with its natural associated purposes of sovereignty of the people, literacy, the embodiment of a fair government that breeds investors' confidence toward a healthy business subsystem in society. Such governance can provide for secure defense as well.
- A disposition for enlightened thinking—the way of thinking that is free, open, objective, and tolerant versus a thinking that is self-centered and unduly traditional.
- The Scottish put it simply and beneficially: leaders must manifest high morals and manners.
- Resistance to existing restrictive ways is a natural right, is in order and is essential.
- The new governance structure must provide for adequate checks and balances among the entities of the government.

- The constructive roles of commerce and property must be embraced.
- Underpinning these factors and others that inescapably will be obliged has to be a short, clear, simple constitution. For length and example of limited, essential content, the U.S. Constitution is a favorable model.

These ten principles are not totally comprehensive, but even if just these were acted upon effectively by a well-intentioned citizenry, there would be a heartening spread of hope and well-being in that renewed nation. If a couple of nations were similarly and fruitfully engaged, it might be contagious.

How to make that first sale or two will be a puzzle. I am likely to be a dissatisfier to the reader for the admitted incompleteness of a how-to recipe.

However, our two role model countries didn't have a complete plan either. Those early handful of Scottish just "dared to start to do something." In time, their following was abundant. Most colonists were not of the mind for independence until it was virtually thrust upon them by a handful of patriots. Then they, the followers, vied to join in the leading.

As wishful as this really is, wouldn't it be advantageous if a handful of change agents in one need-to-change country (maybe even a second, also) would read a book like this and catch a spark.

All right, that is unlikely, but private citizens from the United States, Scotland, Norway, Poland, India, or wherever could self-organize thoughtfully to be alert for the potential of the lighting of such a spark.

Could they, like the Scottish, found a "club," a Founder's Club, from which to knowledgeably encourage, even guide that flicker to brighten?

That could energize another historic enlightenment!

View of the High Street of Edinburgh
from the East, 1793

A Final Word

The Dimming Lights Live On

A next generation of the Scottish Enlightenment was not to be regenerated for inbred and external reasons.

Just at the epic time, the 1770s and 1780s, when the Enlightenment wisdom was clarifying issues, strengthening convictions, and adding a last word for our founders, the light was beginning to dim for their mentors. Striving over two and a half centuries, they had reached an intellectual pinnacle with unparalleled international standing.

The Calvinist thesis of predetermination was becoming deeply ingrained, affecting the mental conduct of many of the well-educated thinkers. More and more, initiative thinking was muting throughout the community. Even if only marginally infecting, it was infective. Higher excellence or even sustained excellence of vectorial thought process was blunted for an interruptive time, leading up to and following 1800.

Even if the Calvin effect had not occurred, new, powerful, and disquieting political, military, economic, and philosophical phenomena were stirring in England and the continent by the early nineteenth century. A continuing Scottish-driven intellectual renaissance was to be at least distractible.

The problem that stimulated the two and a half centuries of generational intellectual growth—search for morals and manners in leadership—was being solved, and many satisfactions from the circa 1750 achievements could be self-satisfying in Scotland.

But finally, Scotland was no longer its own land. The interest of scholars was inevitably partially attracted to its now-joint-kingdom neighbor to the south as well as the continent and even a newly founded America.

And so another inevitable lifecycle was played out. In this case, fortunately, it played long enough for what became our continuing greater good.

Index

A

B

C

Calvin, John 35
Calvinism 32
  principle of predetermination
    107
Campbell, George 54
character, try-to and to-do 20, 44
Charles-Louis de Secondat. *See*
    Montesquieu
checks and balances, system of
    90, 102
Christian humanism. *See*
    Erasmus, Desiderius
colonists 34, 56, 57, 66, 69, 78,
    101, 103
Columbus, Christopher 16
"Common Sense" (Paine) 79
Constitutional Convention 66,
    90
Continental Congress 72
Cosmographiae introductio
    (Waldseemüller) 16
Cullen, William 51, 98

D

Dalrymple, James 41

Declaration of Independence 7,
    8, 71, 78, 79
Descartes, Rene 40
disrespect of freedom 102
divine right of monarchs 32

E

Edinburgh 54, 61, 70 *See*
    "Athens of the North"
  prominence in medicine 41
  the Philosophical Society 62
  the Scots in 37
  University of Edinburgh 27, 40
Erasmus, Desiderius
  Christian Humanism 35
Erksine, John 54

F

Federalist Papers 8
Ferguson, Adam 51, 72, 73
Founding Fathers 54, 89, 91
    See individual Founding
    Father
  lessons from the
    Enlightenment 66, 68
Franklin, Benjamin 56, 80